BUILDINGS AT WORK

Skyscrapers

ELIZABETH ENCARNACION

QEB Publishing

Library of Congress Control Number: 2006038444

ISBN 978 1 59566 371 9

Written by Elizabeth Encarnacion
Designed by Rahul Dhiman (Q2A Media)
Series Editor Honor Head
Foldout illustration by Ian Naylor
Picture Researcher Lalit K Dalal/Rituparna Sengupta

Publisher Steve Evans
Creative Director Zeta Davies
Senior Editor Hannah Ray

Printed and bound in China

Picture credits
Key: T = top, B = bottom, C = center, L = left, R = right, FC = front cover

Zina Seletskaya/ **Shutterstock**: 4–5 (background), Walter Hodges/**CORBIS**: 5t, TIM GRAHAM / **Alamy**: 5b,
Photo Researchers, Inc./ Photolibrary: 6–7 (background), AMERICAN MEMORY/**Library of Congress**: 7t,
Geoffrey Taunton; Cordaiy Photo Library Ltd./**CORBIS**: 7b, Yueh-Hua Lee Photography: 8–9 (background), Lynn
Watson/ **Shutterstock**: 9t, Louie Psihoyos/**CORBIS**: 9b, **Courtesy of Skidmore, Owings & Merrill LLP**:
10–11 (background), **www.burjdubaiskyscraper.com**: 11t, **Kohn Pedersen Fox Associates, East China
Architectural Design & Research Institute Co. Ltd.**: 11b, Animals Animals / Earth Scenes/ **Photolibrary**:
12–13 (background), photooiasson/ **Shutterstock**: 13t, Bill Bachmann Photography/ **Photolibrary**: 13b, Aleksejs
Kostins/ **Shutterstock**: 14–15 (background), pmphoto/ **Shutterstock**: 15t, Index Stock Imagery/ **Photolibrary**:
15b, Susmit Dey Photography, **photographersdirect.com**: 16–17 (background), Mauritius Die Bildagentur Gmbh/
Photolibrary: 20, wong chi kin/ **Shutterstock**: 22, **Courtesy of British Land**: 23t, Madeleine Openshaw/
Shutterstock: 23b, tamir niv/ **Shutterstock**: 24, Stephen A. Edwards: 25t, Ed Parker/**CFW Images/EASI-
Images**: 25b, Workbook, Inc./ **Photolibrary**: 26–27 (background), Paul S. Wolf/ **Shutterstock**: 27t, Julian
Nieman / **Alamy**: 27b, Wilfried Krecichwost/zefa/**CORBIS**: 28–29 (background), Jarno Gonzalez Zarraonandia/
Shutterstock: 29t, Ritu Manoj Jethani/ **Shutterstock**: 29b, Pierre Mens/**HSB Malmö**: 30–31 (background),
Fabian Photography: 31t, Rosewood Hotels and Resorts: 31b, **glasgow.architecture.co.uk**: 33t.

Words in bold can be found in the Glossary on page 34.

Web site information is correct at time of going to press. However, the publishers
cannot accept liability for any information or links found on third-party Web sites.

CONTENTS

SKYSCRAPERS

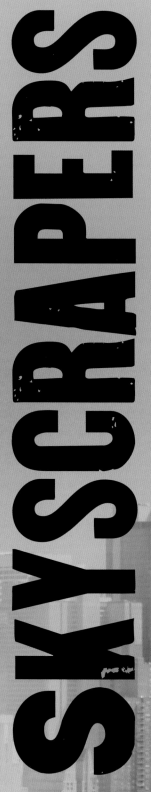

A skyscraper is a very tall building in which people live or work. To people walking on the street below, a skyscraper's top is so high it seems to touch, or scrape, the sky. Different people have different ideas about what makes a building a skyscraper. Some people say that a skyscraper must be around 500 feet (150 meters) tall. Others think it should just be much taller than the buildings around it. Either way, only the very tallest high-rise buildings are called skyscrapers.

▼ Many big cities are filled with skyscrapers, which provide more space for people to live and work.

The steel revolution

Constructing buildings taller than ten **stories** was almost impossible until the mid-1800s, when **engineers** discovered how to produce large quantities of **steel**—a material that was far lighter than brick, but very strong. Brick buildings with more than a few stories required the lower floors to have thick walls to support all the extra weight of the floors above. Steel meant that the walls could be the same thickness throughout the whole building, making it easier to build higher.

▲ Tall skyscrapers would not be possible without strong steel beams.

▼ The Chrysler Building's roof has lights that make it shine at night.

MAKE IT PRETTY

Architects **often add decorative touches when they are designing** skyscrapers. The Chrysler Building in New York City was built in the 1920s as the headquarters for the Chrysler car company. The architect decided to change his plans to make some of the decoration on the building look like parts of a car. The spire **and roof were covered with shiny** stainless steel, **and large copies of** hood ornaments **and** radiator caps **were used as decorations and** gargoyles.

EARLY SKYSCRAPERS

In the early 1900s, builders in New York City were racing to be the first to construct the tallest skyscrapers in the world. The race to build the tallest building became so competitive that the architect of the Chrysler Building announced a false height for his design. Soon after, the Manhattan Company skyscraper was declared the tallest building in the world. Then, in 1930, the architect installed the spire on top of the Chrysler Building and stole the title. The next year, the Empire State Building was finished at a height of 1,453 feet (443 meters) and remained the world's tallest building for 41 years.

Many early skyscrapers, such ➤ as the Empire State Building, are still used today.

The first skyscraper

Compared with modern skyscrapers, the first high-rise buildings seem tiny. However, early skyscrapers such as the Home Insurance Building in Chicago, Illinois, were the first to use steel columns and **beams** to make the structures lighter so they could be thinner and taller. This **technology** is still used today to make skyscrapers reach the sky.

The Home Insurance Building ▶ was built in 1885. It was only twelve stories tall, but it was the first skyscraper.

BEFORE SKYSCRAPERS

When it was completed in 1873, the Midland Grand Hotel (now known as St. Pancras Chambers) in London, England, was the largest hotel in the world. It used many of the new ideas that helped make the first skyscrapers possible. Concrete **was used to make the floors strong and fireproof.** Hydraulic ascending rooms, an early type of elevator, were installed to help hotel guests reach their rooms more easily.

◀ The clock tower on St. Pancras Chambers is 269 feet (82 meters) tall.

THE WORLD'S TALLEST

Most experts consider Taipei 101, built in 2004, to be the world's tallest building.

In 1998, the Petronas Towers in Kuala Lumpur, Malaysia, claimed the title of the world's tallest building because its spires were taller than the roof of the Sears Tower in Chicago. However, the Sears Tower had **antennae** that were even taller than the Petronas Towers' spire, so it claimed it was still the tallest. To solve the argument, an international group of engineers created four categories of tallest buildings. The first category is for the building that is tallest from the ground floor to the top of the spire. The second is for the building with the highest floor where people live or work. The third category is for the building that is the tallest from its ground floor to its roof, and the fourth is for the building that is tallest from the ground floor to the top of the antenna. Taiwan's Taipei 101 is now at the top in the first three categories, but the Sears Tower still has the tallest antenna.

ANTENNA ANTICS

With its tallest antenna reaching 283 feet (86.3 meters) above its roof, the Sears Tower is the tallest skyscraper measured from its base to the top of its antenna. The Sears Tower actually has two antennae—the shorter one measures 253 feet (77 meters). The antennae are lit up in different colors at different times of the year. In March, the antennae are lit green for St. Patrick's Day. In October, they are orange for Halloween, and in December they are red and green for Christmas.

▲ Airplane warning lights at the top of the Sears Tower's two antennae flash 40 times a minute.

Going up

Double-decker elevators in Taipei 101 can carry twice as many people to higher floors without taking up more room in the **vertical core**. These express elevators take workers directly to a **sky lobby** on a much higher floor where they can change to another elevator to reach the floors above that point. The lobbies are also double-decker, and usually have escalators running between the paired floors.

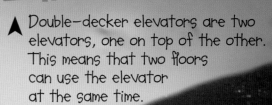

▲ Double-decker elevators are two elevators, one on top of the other. This means that two floors can use the elevator at the same time.

FACT!

Taipei 101's double-decker express elevators can travel at 39 miles (63 kilometers) per hour!

SUPER SKYSCRAPERS

Just as New York architects raced to construct the tallest skyscrapers in the early 1900s, today's skyscrapers are being built higher and higher to break the record. Having the world's tallest building can give a city, or even an entire country, a strong sense of pride and attract tourists to visit in greater numbers. In fact, there are many superskyscrapers currently being planned or built that could become the world's tallest in one or more category. The Freedom Tower, being built at the site of the World Trade Center in New York City, was designed with an antenna that will reach 1,776 feet (541.3 meters). The number 1776 symbolizes the year that America declared its independence.

This image shows what the New York City skyline might look like once the Freedom Tower is built. ➤

FACT!

It will take three to four months to clean all the windows of the completed Burj Dubai.

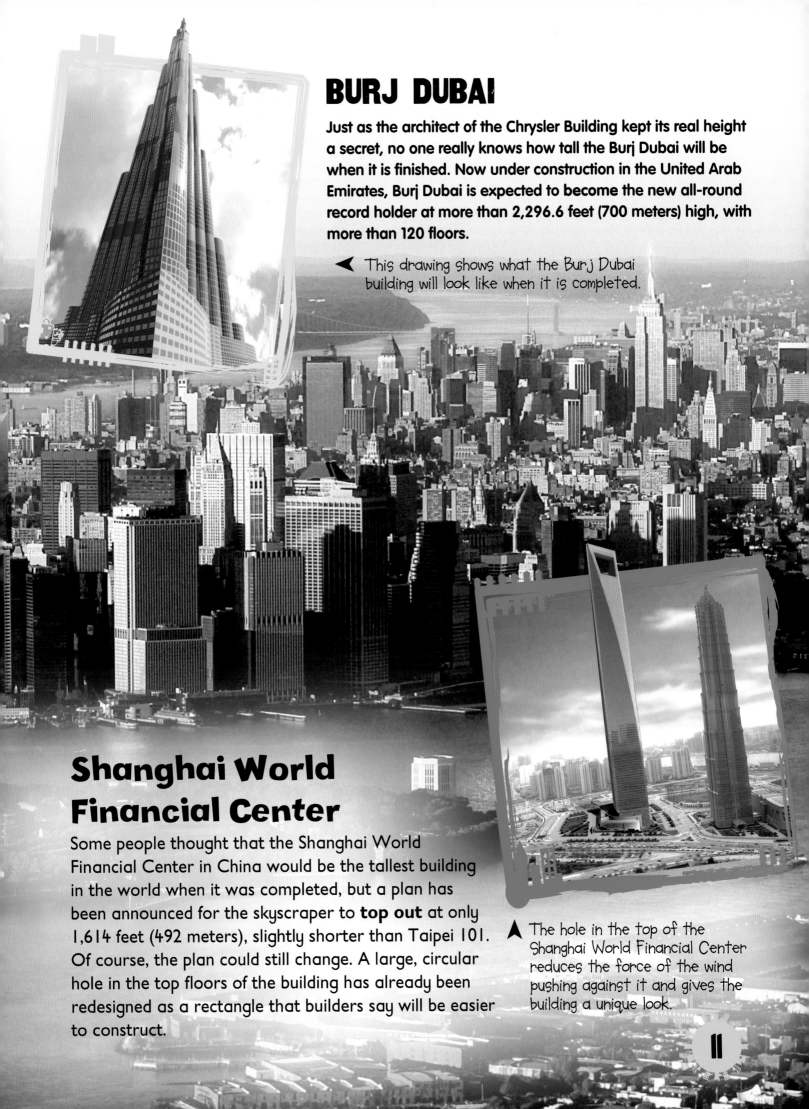

BURJ DUBAI

Just as the architect of the Chrysler Building kept its real height a secret, no one really knows how tall the Burj Dubai will be when it is finished. Now under construction in the United Arab Emirates, Burj Dubai is expected to become the new all-round record holder at more than 2,296.6 feet (700 meters) high, with more than 120 floors.

◄ This drawing shows what the Burj Dubai building will look like when it is completed.

Shanghai World Financial Center

Some people thought that the Shanghai World Financial Center in China would be the tallest building in the world when it was completed, but a plan has been announced for the skyscraper to **top out** at only 1,614 feet (492 meters), slightly shorter than Taipei 101. Of course, the plan could still change. A large, circular hole in the top floors of the building has already been redesigned as a rectangle that builders say will be easier to construct.

▲ The hole in the top of the Shanghai World Financial Center reduces the force of the wind pushing against it and gives the building a unique look.

TWIN TOWERS

Sometimes it is easier to build two skyscrapers instead of one huge building that could hold the same number of people. As buildings become taller, the **central core** that contains the elevators, emergency stairs, and other services takes up a greater area. That means less room is available on each floor for work or living space. Offices in a building that is wider and deeper are more likely to be without windows. However, with twin skyscrapers, such as the Petronas Towers in Kuala Lumpur, more workers can fit in a small area with plenty of natural light.

The Petronas Towers ➤ are the tallest twin towers in the world.

FACT!

The Petronas Towers are connected by a two-level bridge at the 41st and 42nd floors that allows people to cross from one building into the other. It has expansion joints that allow the towers to move slightly without damaging the bridge.

Leaning towers

Most leaning towers lean because they're starting to fall down. However, the twin towers of the Puerta de Europa in Madrid, Spain, were built to lean toward each other. The architect wanted to design two buildings that would form a gateway. ("Puerta" means gateway in Spanish.) These twin towers are so similar that their **helipads** had to be painted different colors so helicopter pilots could tell them apart from the air!

▲ Each of these towers leans three times as much as the Leaning Tower of Pisa, in Italy.

NEW YORK'S TWIN TOWERS

The World Trade Center in New York City was actually a complex of seven high-rise buildings, with the super-tall twin towers as the centerpiece. These famous buildings, which were the tallest in the world when they were completed in 1973, still influence the way skyscrapers are designed, even though they are no longer standing. For example, express elevators with sky lobbies, similar to the ones in Taipei 101, were first in the Twin Towers of the World Trade Center.

◀ The Twin Towers of the World Trade Center solved many problems that had kept skyscrapers from reaching greater heights.

13

STEEL FRAMES

A steel **frame** acts like a person's skeleton, supporting the building and keeping everything in its place. Steel is one of the strongest building materials, but it is light enough to use in very tall buildings without having to add any extra support on the lower floors. However, steel is more expensive than some other construction materials, and it can be damaged by rust or the heat from a fire.

Large cranes are used ➤ to lift the heavy steel beams into place.

CURTAINS

If the steel frame is a skeleton, then the curtain wall is the skin of the skyscraper. A curtain wall does not help to support the weight of the building in the way that a brick wall on a house does. Instead, it covers the frame like a curtain, shielding the people inside the building from natural elements such as rain, heat, and wind. Curtain walls can also be decorative, as on the Empire State Building, which has a classic, limestone-**covered appearance, or on a glass-covered skyscraper with a sleek, modern look.**

The smooth glass walls of many skyscrapers are supported by steel frames. ▶

Hot stuff

After a crane lifts them into place, steel beams are bolted or **welded** together to create a strong, permanent connection. Then, the beams are sprayed with a **fireproof coating** so they will not weaken if a fire starts inside the building.

◀ Welders must wear protective gear, such as welding helmets, goggles, and thick gloves.

Emergency stairs
used when fire or power outs make the elevators unsafe

Concrete core
the strong "backbone." Helps keep the building stable

Elevator shafts
elevators travel up and down inside hollow elevator shafts

Sky lobby
intermediate floors where people can change from an express elevator to another elevator or stairway

Curtain wall
an outer wall that does not support the building

FACT!
The city of Hong Kong has nearly 8,000 skyscrapers.

18

Sky high

Skyscraper construction workers can't be afraid of heights, but they must be careful about safety! Harnesses attached to safety lines keep them from falling off the building, and construction hats protect their heads from anything falling from above. Special temporary elevators on the side of the building carry them up to the top and back down again.

▲ Builders use this elevator on the outside of a skyscraper that is under construction.

Structural top
the highest part of the building that cannot be removed

Antenna
the height helps transmit radio or television waves further without other buildings blocking them

Ventilation systems
provide clean air and move it around the building

Tuned mass damper
computers move a heavy weight from side to side to keep the skyscraper from swaying in strong winds

REINFORCED CONCRETE

Concrete poured around ➤
steel rods is a cheaper
building method than
using steel frames.

Concrete
is made from
water, cement, and
gravel or sand. Concrete is very
strong against forces that squeeze
it together (such as gravity pulling
down on it), but not as strong
when forces bend it (such as wind
pushing on a skyscraper). To make it
stronger against these forces, builders
reinforce the concrete by pouring it
over a grid of small steel rods and letting
it dry. Reinforced concrete is very cheap
to produce. The concrete can take a long
time to dry, which slows down construction,
but new, fast-drying concretes are being
developed to solve that problem.

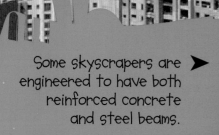
Some skyscrapers are engineered to have both reinforced concrete and steel beams. ➤

THE BACKBONE

Many modern skyscrapers are built with a hollow concrete core surrounded by steel framing. This method produces a lighter, more open, steel-frame construction while at the same time giving the building a strong backbone that can help keep it steady. The concrete core contains the elevator shafts, **emergency stairs,** air ducts, **and other** central services.

FACT!

The CITIC Plaza in Guangzhou, China, is the tallest concrete building in the world at 1,282.8 feet (391 meters).

A good foundation

Foundations act like the feet of the skyscraper. They support the weight of everything above them and spread that weight out across the ground below. First, columns made from steel or reinforced concrete are placed into holes in the **bedrock** or deep soil. Then, the construction workers insert steel **reinforcing rods** and pour concrete around the rods and the columns to make strong foundations. The steel or reinforced concrete frame of the building is then connected to the foundations.

▲ Diggers make holes in the bedrock for the foundations of a skyscraper.

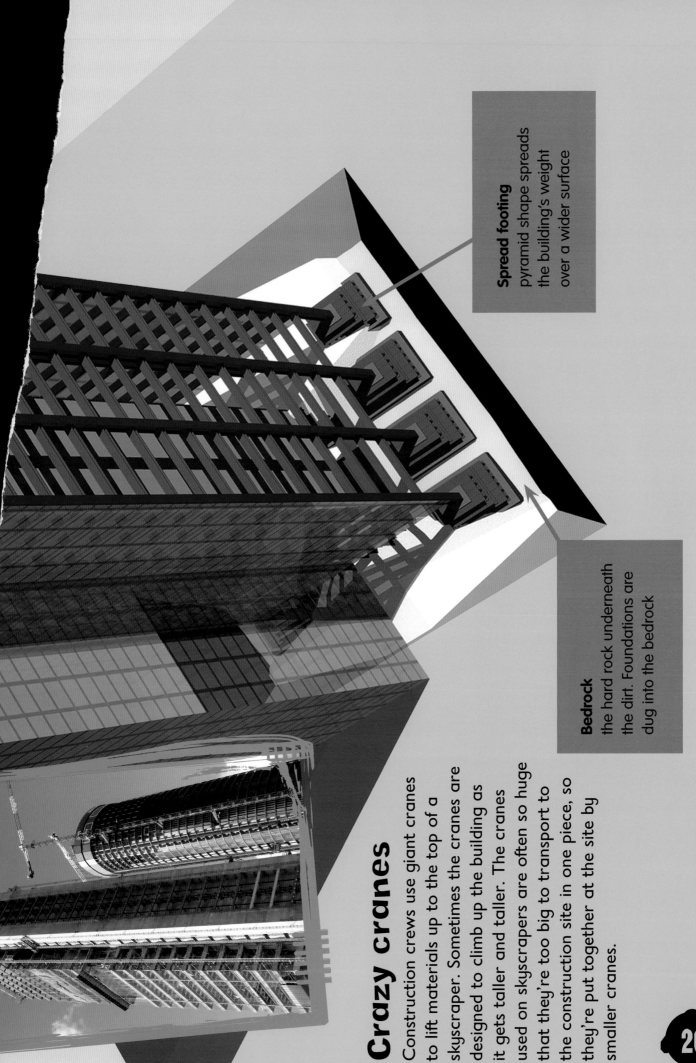

Spread footing
pyramid shape spreads
the building's weight
over a wider surface

Bedrock
the hard rock underneath
the dirt. Foundations are
dug into the bedrock

Crazy cranes

Construction crews use giant cranes
to lift materials up to the top of a
skyscraper. Sometimes the cranes are
designed to climb up the building as
it gets taller and taller. The cranes
used on skyscrapers are often so huge
that they're too big to transport to
the construction site in one piece, so
they're put together at the site by
smaller cranes.

Office floor
may be large open areas like this, or separated into smaller rooms

Steel frame
the inner "skeleton" of a skyscraper that gives it its shape

▶ Large skyscrapers often need more than one crane to lift all the construction materials.

CROSS–BRACING

The triangles on the outer walls of this building give it strength against natural forces. ►

Wind pushes against skyscrapers with great force and can make them sway back and forth. The people working or living inside might feel uncomfortable, or even sick, if the building was moving all the time. Adding diagonal braces to the outside of the skyscraper can help strengthen the structure against the wind. I.M. Pei, a famous architect, designed the Bank of China Tower in Hong Kong so that the **cross-bracing** would be a part of the outer wall and the skyscraper thought of as a working piece of art.

RADICAL RAFT

Architects planning the Broadgate Tower in London, England, faced a unique problem: The skyscraper was to be built on a concrete and steel raft over a train tunnel. This meant that the foundation could not support the weight of a concrete core. Instead, the architects designed a cross-braced outer wall that would support the structure, while strengthening the building against the forces of gravity and wind.

The Broadgate Tower was designed with cross-bracing that makes it light, but strong. ➤

▼ Each X-shape on the outer walls of the John Hancock Center is between 16 and 18 stories tall.

X marks the spot

Chicago, Illinois, is often called the Windy City. High-rise construction workers had to come up with ways of protecting their buildings from the strong winds that are common in the city. Cross-bracing was used to prevent the John Hancock Center from being moved around by the powerful wind. The giant X-shapes on the outside of the building mean fewer support beams were needed on the inside. More of the interior of the building could therefore be used for work and living spaces without large columns getting in the way.

FIGHTING NATURE

Some skyscrapers are built in places where earthquakes and hurricanes are common. Powerful, sudden forces pushing against the sides of a building could damage it, so architects study the effects of these natural forces and find ways of keeping the structure steady. The Jin Mao Tower in Shanghai, China, has a strong concrete core that acts like a backbone, keeping it stiff even in a strong earthquake or the 125 mph (200 kmph) winds of a major typhoon.

◄ At 1,381 feet (421 meters) tall, the Jin Mao Tower has many systems to stop it from swaying in the wind.

Earthquake-proof

Mexico City is right in the center of one of the world's most active earthquake zones. Designers had to use the most up-to-date technology to fight the forces of earthquakes while building the Torre Mayor, the tallest building in Latin America. One system uses 98 giant **shock absorbers** to reduce the movement of the building and its parts.

WILD WIND

Some skyscrapers, such as the Citicorp Center in New York and Taipei 101 in Taiwan, use a tuned mass damper to reduce movement caused by wind. Taipei 101's damper is a 660 ton ball. When the building leans one way, the ball slowly starts to follow, but by that time the building is already trying to lean back the other way. The mass of the ball is so great that it pulls the building back toward the center, reducing the movement.

Some skyscrapers have a large ▶ weight in their upper floors to slow down the building's movement.

FACT!

The swimming pool on the 57th floor of the Jin Mao Tower acts as a damper to reduce the building's movement in strong winds!

◀ 1,700 construction workers helped to build the Torre Mayor in Mexico City.

EXTREME TEMPERATURES

When planning a new skyscraper, an architect must think about the weather in that location. Very hot or very cold temperatures may create problems that the architect must remember in his or her design. The Burj Al Arab, which is located on a man-made island just off the coast of Dubai in the United Arab Emirates, is the tallest hotel building in the world at 1,053 feet (321 meters). Its windows face the cooler water out at sea, while a special **fiberglass fabric** on the side facing the desert coast helps repel heat and provide soft, filtered light inside.

◄ The Burj Al Arab's shape was inspired by an Arabian sailing ship.

LET IT SNOW

One Liberty Place in Philadelphia, Pennsylvania, has a sloping, tiered roof that could become dangerous for the people walking below if snow or ice collected on it. As a result, this skyscraper was designed with a system that melts the ice and snow off the outside walls before it can become a problem.

Skyscrapers in cold areas must protect people on the sidewalk below from falling snow and ice. ➤

FACT!

The Al Faisaliah Center in the desert city of Riyadh, Saudi Arabia, freezes as many as 110,231 lbs. (50,000 kg) of ice each night. The building's cooling system lets the ice melt during the day to help chill the air.

◀ Outer walls without windows can help keep a building cooler.

Hot, hot, hot

In the hot desert climate of Jeddah, Saudi Arabia, an outer wall of windows would make it very difficult to keep the building cool. The National Commerce Bank was designed with most of the windows facing in toward a central **atrium**. Three large holes in the building's outer wall allow indirect sunlight to filter into the offices, providing natural light without too much heat. Gardens growing in the open areas created by the large holes mean office workers have an attractive view.

27

GREEN SKYSCRAPERS

Today's builders are working hard to make their skyscrapers "green." These buildings are not painted green, but are designed to save energy and use fewer **natural resources**. Some even bring the outdoors inside. The Commerzbank Tower in Frankfurt, Germany, has nine "sky gardens" spread throughout the building. Each office in the skyscraper has a view of either the city or an indoor garden. Natural light hits every office window, which means that workers do not need to use so many artificial lights and therefore need less electricity. The open areas inside the building create natural airflow, reducing the costs of **air conditioning**.

Many buildings, like the Commerzbank Tower, (right) use natural light, ventilation shafts, and indoor gardens to save energy.

The Gherkin

30 St. Mary Axe in London, England, is also known as "the Gherkin" because of its unusual shape. Many of the construction materials used in the structure were either recycled, or designed to be reused in the future. The building's design also helps to save energy by reducing the need for artificial light, heating, and air conditioning. For example, the Gherkin's distinctive **tinted** glass reduces the amount of heat absorbed by the building, making it cooler.

The Gherkin uses only half the energy a traditional skyscraper of its size would use. ➤

FULL OF ENERGY

The Condé Nast Building at 4 Times Square is famous for being the first environmentally friendly skyscraper in New York. Fuel cells **and** solar panels in the building help reduce the amount of electricity needed from outside sources. A state-of-the-art system filters the air, making it a healthier environment in which to work. Recycling chutes deliver reusable waste to storage areas, where it is picked up and taken to recycling centers.

◄ The curtain wall of the Condé Nast Building shades and **insulates** the offices inside so less heating or air conditioning is needed.

SPECIAL SKYSCRAPERS

Architects have to keep many things in mind while they are designing new skyscrapers. City **building codes**, strong natural forces, and what the building will be used for are all important factors to consider. But, the architect also wants the building to look good and attract attention. The HSB Turning Torso building in Sweden looks like a giant work of art because the architect copied the shape of a sculpture that he had created in the past. When it was built, it was the only "twisting" skyscraper in the world, but it has already inspired new skyscraper designs in other countries.

The HSB Turning Torso skyscraper ➤ is made up of nine "cubes" that appear to twist around the central core.

FACT!

Cranes could not be used during construction of the Turning Torso because of its curving design. Instead, the building's elevators were installed in stages to haul the construction materials up to the higher floors.

BUILDING BLOCKS

The Nakagin Capsule Tower in Tokyo, Japan, was built with 140 individual apartments, or capsules, all stacked in different directions and attached to a central concrete core. Each capsule has its own furniture and appliances built into the walls. Televisions, radios, and even calculators have been installed. The units were designed so they could be easily taken apart to be modernized or replaced.

◀ Each apartment in the Nakagin Capsule Tower was constructed at a factory before being lifted into place by a large crane and bolted to the concrete core.

Around the globe

A large, golden sphere sits just below the spire of the Al Faisaliah Center in Riyadh, Saudi Arabia. This tinted glass-covered bubble has a multilevel restaurant inside, allowing diners to enjoy amazing views of the city in every direction.

▶ The Al Faisaliah Center may have been designed to remind people of a ballpoint pen.

TALL TOWERS

Skyscrapers are not the tallest structures in the world. In fact, many towers, such as the CN Tower in Toronto, Canada, reach higher into the sky than the tallest skyscrapers. The CN Tower is the world's tallest freestanding structure on land, but it is not considered a skyscraper because it is not a place for people to live or work around the clock. Some **communications** towers, often called masts, are built even taller, so that radio and television signals can reach more homes. They are supported by wires that stop them from falling down.

At 1,815.3 feet (553.3 meters) ➤ tall, the CN Tower is taller than the world's tallest skyscraper.

▲ The tall Glasgow Tower has a motor that can rotate it into the wind.

Going round in circles

The Glasgow Tower at the Glasgow Science Center in Scotland is the only building in the world that can turn in circles. The tower is shaped like an airplane's wing, which reduces the force of the wind on the structure. To work properly, the wing shape must face into the wind, so the tower's base has a motor that can turn it in any direction.

air conditioning A system that spreads cooled air throughout a building

air ducts Hollow metal tubes through which air flows from one place to another, often used in heating and air conditioning systems

antennae Metal rods that send or receive radio waves

architects People who design buildings and oversee their construction

atrium An open area inside a building that extends upward for several stories

beams Strong pieces of metal or wood used as a support in a building

bedrock The solid layer of rock beneath the dirt or sand on Earth's surface

building codes Rules and laws that builders follow during construction to make buildings safe

capsules An apartment that is made in a factory, then transported to the building site to be installed

central core A strong column in the center of a skyscraper that surrounds the elevators and stairways and supports the building. Also called the vertical core

central services The basic service and supply systems of a building, such as elevators, stairways, garbage chutes, and lobbies

communications A system for passing information from one place to another, such as telephones

complex A group of buildings connected by passageways or underground tunnels

concrete A very strong construction material made by mixing water and cement with gravel or sand

cross-bracing Diagonal beams used to support the structure of a building and reduce movement

curtain wall An outside wall that does not help support the weight of a building

elevator shafts Hollow passages inside a building in which an elevator travels up and down

engineers People who design machines or other technology

fiberglass fabric A very strong fabric made from fine glass fibers

fireproof coating A material that covers steel beams and makes them more difficult to damage with fire

frame The structure underneath the outer surface of a building that gives it strength

fuel cells Devices that change chemical energy into electricity without much waste or pollution

gargoyles Sculptures, often in the shape of a strange-looking human or animal, designed to drain rainwater away from a building

helipad A hard surface from which helicopters can take off or land

hood ornaments Metallic decorations on the front of a car, often shaped like an animal

hydraulic ascending rooms Early types of elevator moved by pressurized liquid

insulates Protects from the weather and extreme temperatures

limestone A rock, often used in building, that is mostly made up of shells and the skeletons of marine life

natural resources Useful materials that are found in nature, such as trees and fresh water

radiator caps Round, metallic lids that close the container of water that cools the engine of a car

raft A type of foundation with supports like a bridge. A raft allows architects to construct buildings on soft earth or uneven land

reinforcing rods Used to give a building strength and support

shock absorbers Devices that absorb sudden bursts of energy, such as earthquake tremors, to reduce the up-and-down movement of a building

sky lobby A public floor halfway up a high-rise building where people can change from one set of elevators to another

solar panels Flat sheets of glass that turn solar energy (sunlight) into electricity

spire A pointed roof or thin projection on the top of a building

stainless steel A combination of two metals, which does not rust easily

steel A strong metal construction material

stories Levels or floors of a building

technology The study of how to solve everyday problems with tools

tiered roof A roof with layers that slope upward in a step-like pattern

tinted Partially shaded, like sunglasses

top out To reach the highest point of construction on a skyscraper

tuned mass damper A device that absorbs energy from strong forces to reduce the side-to-side movement of a building

vertical core A strong column in the center of a skyscraper that surrounds the elevators and stairways and supports the building

welded When pieces of metal are joined together using extreme heat to melt them. The pieces are pushed together until the metal cools and hardens

welders Construction workers who use heat to join pieces of metal together

FIND OUT MORE

Web sites

Learn more about the forces that push against a skyscraper:
www.pbs.org/wgbh/buildingbig/skyscraper/index.html

Watch an animation of Taipei 101's tuned mass damper at work:
www.motioneering.ca/Public/Taipei101Animation.aspx

Get more information about specific buildings
www.emporis.com
Click on "buildings" in the blue bar.

Take a virtual skyscraper tour of New York City
www.skyscraper.org/webwalk/map4.html